WILD WHEELS

MUSTANGS

By Michael Portman

Gareth Stevens
Publishing

Please visit our Web site, www.garethstevens.com. For a free color catalog of all our high-quality books, call toll free 1-800-542-2595 or fax 1-877-542-2596.

Library of Congress Cataloging-in-Publication Data

Portman, Michael, 1976-
  Mustangs / Michael Portman.
     p. cm. – (Wild wheels)
  Includes index.
  ISBN 978-1-4339-4752-0 (pbk.)
  ISBN 978-1-4339-4753-7 (6-pack)
  ISBN 978-1-4339-4751-3 (library binding)
  1. Mustang automobile—Juvenile literature. I. Title.
  TL215.M8P67 2011
  629.222'2–dc22

                                        2010037587

First Edition

Published in 2011 by
Gareth Stevens Publishing
111 East 14th Street, Suite 349
New York, NY 10003

Copyright © 2011 Gareth Stevens Publishing

Designer: Christopher Logan
Editor: Therese Shea

Photo credits: Cover, p. 1 (Mustang) iStockphoto/Thinkstock; cover, pp. 1–3 (background), 30–32 (background), 2–32 (flame border), back cover (engine), 10, 11, 12–13, 18–19, 28–29 Shutterstock.com; pp. 4–5 FPG/Getty Images; pp. 6, 7, 21 Car Culture/Getty Images; pp. 8–9 Ben Martin/Time & Life Pictures/Getty Images; pp. 14, 15 iStockphoto.com; pp. 16–17, 22–23, © Kimball Stock Photo; pp. 24–25 Bryan Mitchell/Getty Images; pp. 26–27 Bryan Haraway/Bloomberg via Getty Images.

Printed in the United States of America

CPSIA compliance information: Batch #CW11GS: For further information contact Gareth Stevens, New York, New York at 1-800-542-2595.

CONTENTS

Words in the glossary appear in **bold** type the first time they are used in the text.

A Good Idea

In the early 1960s, European sports cars were very popular in the United States. Unlike big, boxy American cars, European sports cars were small and curvy. The Ford Motor Company didn't see the popularity of European sports cars as a danger, but as an opportunity. What if they made their own sports car?

This photo was taken as an ad for the Ford Mustang. It suggested the car was sporty, but good for families.

Instead of making a two-seater like the ones from Europe, Ford decided to add a backseat. This made the car more practical. Ford also knew that the car would have to be both good-looking and affordable to be successful. The result was the Ford Mustang, introduced in April 1964.

INSIDE THE MACHINE

Some said the Ford Mustang was named after the P-51 Mustang, a small World War II fighter plane. However, the **designers** at Ford decided to connect the car to a different image. Since a mustang is also a horse that was once wild in the American West, the designers used a horse as the car's **emblem**.

A New Breed

The Ford Mustang introduced the world to a new class of automobile called the "pony car." A pony car is a small, sporty car with a powerful engine. Although the Ford Mustang wasn't the first car to fit this label, its popularity set the standard for what a pony car should be.

Pony cars often weren't as powerful as their larger **muscle-car** cousins. This is because larger cars have room for bigger engines with more horsepower, the measurement of an engine's power. Since not everyone who wanted a powerful car also wanted a big car, the pony car was the perfect answer.

Ford Mustangs were associated with a fun, young crowd. Here a group of surfers pose with their 1965 Mustang.

INSIDE THE MACHINE

The Plymouth Barracuda came out **2** weeks before the Mustang, but it wasn't nearly as successful. The name "pony car" comes from the Ford Mustang's horse emblem. Had the Barracuda been more successful, pony cars might have been called fish cars!

engine of 1964½ Ford Mustang

Off and Running

Before the Mustang was unveiled at the 1964 World's Fair in New York City, Ford worked hard to build excitement. New cars are usually introduced in the fall, so Ford had an advantage by offering the Mustang in the spring. Without other cars competing for attention, the Mustang had the spotlight to itself. Ford used publicity stunts and television and print ads to make the Mustang the most awaited car of the year.

Ford's plan worked perfectly. The Mustang was an instant hit. Ford sold 22,000 Mustangs on the first day! Within a year, 417,000 Mustangs were sold.

As a crowd at the 1964 World's Fair watches, a family takes a ride in the first model of the Ford Mustang.

INSIDE THE MACHINE

The Mustang was a hit with children, too. A pedal-powered toy Mustang was one of the most popular Christmas gifts in 1964. More than 93,000 were sold. For those a little older, there was the "Mustang Jr.," a minicar powered by gas or a battery. The gas-powered version could reach speeds of 20 miles (32 km) per hour, while the battery-powered version traveled at a much safer 5 miles (8 km) per hour.

Ford

Building a Legend

In order to make the Mustang affordable, Ford used a common practice called **platform sharing**. This allows automobile manufacturers to quickly and inexpensively build new cars by using many of the same parts and structures as existing models. The first generation, or class, of Mustang was built using the same platform as Ford's smallest car, the Falcon. The Mustang, however, was a completely different animal.

The Mustang's body featured sculpted lines and folds. The taillights were divided into three sections on each side. But the most noticeable feature was the emblem of the galloping horse on the **grille**.

The headlights of the first Mustang model were round, as if the car was wide-eyed and ready for action!

INSIDE THE MACHINE

The first Mustang rolled out of the factory just 18 months after it was designed. That's much quicker than most cars. Cars go through different design changes before they're ready to be built. Today, it can take several years before a new car goes from the design stage to the showroom floor. Sometimes, it never gets made at all.

Ford Mustang grille and emblem

Since the Mustang was issued months before the usual production year, the Mustangs made during this time period are often called 1964½ models. Still others call these cars "early 1965s" and the cars built the next year "late 1965s." However, Ford classified the 1964½ Mustangs as 1965 models.

Originally, the Mustang was only offered as a **coupe** or **convertible**. For the 1965 model year, Ford introduced a type with a rear roofline that sloped towards the trunk, called a fastback. Customers looking for a higher-performance Mustang found it in the Mustang GT (Grand Touring).

INSIDE THE MACHINE

The first Mustangs sold for an average of $2,368. Mustang customers could **customize** their cars by choosing from a long list of options, or choices. The list was longer than for any other Ford car. The priciest single option for the 1965 Mustang was air conditioning—about $280. Rear-seat speakers for the radio were about $12.

OIL

This Mustang coupe was a popular choice in the 1965 Mustang line.

ICE COLD

13

Facing the Competition

By the time Ford introduced the 1966 models in August 1965, they had already sold an amazing number of Mustangs. Ford Mustangs were everywhere—even at the top of the Empire State Building! As a publicity stunt, a 1966 Mustang was assembled on the Empire State Building's 86th-floor observation deck.

This is the Chevrolet Camaro Z28, a popular pony car that never quite reached the popularity of the Mustang.

By 1967, Ford faced serious competition from other companies building their own pony cars. The Chevrolet Camaro, Pontiac Firebird, Plymouth Barracuda, and even the Ford-owned Mercury Cougar got in on the act. However, the Mustang continued to outsell its rivals.

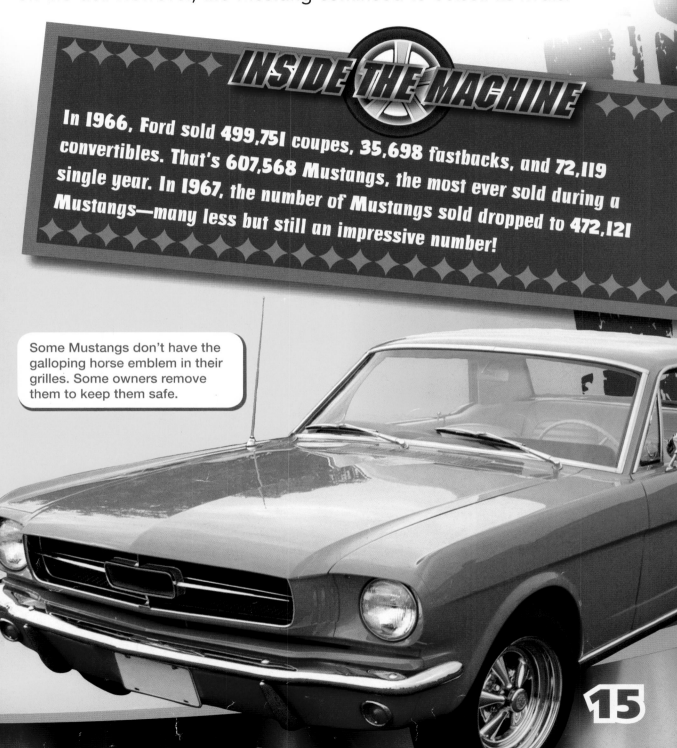

INSIDE THE MACHINE

In 1966, Ford sold 499,751 coupes, 35,698 fastbacks, and 72,119 convertibles. That's 607,568 Mustangs, the most ever sold during a single year. In 1967, the number of Mustangs sold dropped to 472,121 Mustangs—many less but still an impressive number!

Some Mustangs don't have the galloping horse emblem in their grilles. Some owners remove them to keep them safe.

Getting Bigger

From 1967 until 1973, the Mustang got bigger but not necessarily more powerful. In the late 1960s, Ford developed **big-block engines** called the Cobra Jet and the Boss to compete with the other pony cars in road races. The Mustang had success on the track. However, by 1972, the big-block engines were gone.

The Boss 302 Mustang was only made 2 years, 1969 and 1970. This 1970 model could go from 0 to 60 miles (97 km) per hour in under 7 seconds.

The Ford Mustang was no longer the small, powerful car it had been. Increased fuel costs caused cars with powerful engines to fall out of favor with customers. Sales of Mustangs fell dramatically. By 1973, Ford decided to make a change.

INSIDE THE MACHINE

The Boss 429 engine was designed for use in NASCAR (National Association for Stock Car Auto Racing) races. However, Ford entered the Torino model instead of the Mustang. The Boss 302 engine made 1969 Mustangs "near-racers" for street use. Over 1,600 were sold.

Hold Your Horses

The second generation of Mustang—called the Mustang II—is widely considered today to be the most disliked of all Mustangs. However, in 1974, when it was first offered, opinions were very different. Customers had demanded a smaller, more **fuel-efficient** Mustang, and that's exactly what Ford created. Built on the Ford Pinto platform, the **subcompact** Mustang II was underpowered. Some models could get up to 34 miles (55 km) per gallon, though. That's a good number even by today's standards!

As the 1970s drew to a close, fuel prices began to drop. Customers were eager for a sportier, higher-horsepower Mustang again. In 1979, the Mustang II was replaced by an all-new generation.

A Mustang Cobra II was used in the hit TV show *Charlie's Angels*. The Cobra II looked powerful. It was a fastback with racing stripes and front and rear **spoilers**. But, aside from its looks, it was just a regular Mustang II.

The Ford Mustang II had a boxier grille and overall look than past Mustangs.

Fresh Start

The third generation of Mustang lasted from 1979 until 1993 and was built on Ford's Fox platform. It was longer than the Mustang II but shorter than the original. The new Mustang was offered initially as either a coupe or **hatchback** and later as a convertible. In 1982, the Mustang GT returned for the first time in 12 years.

Ford continued to improve the Mustang's engines every year. Once again, the Mustang was a performance car. Ford made relatively few changes to the Mustang's appearance during this generation. The biggest change came in 1987, when Ford smoothed out the Mustang's edges to make it more **aerodynamic**.

INSIDE THE MACHINE

A 1979 Ford Mustang was used as the Indianapolis 500 pace car, the car that leads racers around the track to warm up their engines. Mustangs have been used as pace cars in the Indy 500 three times: 1964, 1979, and 1994. The 1964½ Mustang had been on the market for a month when it became the Indy 500 pace car.

Though it looks much different from the first Mustangs, the 1988 Mustangs sold well. The car was still a great value for its high performance.

Restyled

In 1994, after 15 successful years, Ford introduced a Mustang built on the Fox platform for its fourth generation. It was different from the earlier generation in almost every way. It was sleeker and sportier. The galloping horse emblem, which had been missing for many years, returned to the grille.

In 1999, Ford put out a redesigned Mustang. Sharp lines replaced rounded edges, and creases replaced curves. The Mustang remained popular, with the 2000 model being the first to sell more than 200,000 in a model year since 1989.

The Mustang Saleen, shown here as a 1999 model, was named for race-car driver Steve Saleen. Ford sometimes works with successful drivers to develop better cars.

During the 1970s, convertibles weren't popular. Most auto manufacturers stopped making them. The convertibles that were sold were usually hardtops that had been modified into convertibles by other companies. The 1994 Mustang convertible was the first Mustang since 1973 that was designed and built as a convertible.

21st-Century Muscle

In 2005, Ford unveiled the fifth-generation Mustang. Built on an all-new platform—the D2C—the new design was heavily affected by the 1967, 1968, and 1969 Mustang models. It looked both modern and old-fashioned at the same time. Ford's design chief called the style "retro-futurism." "Retro" means modeled on the past. In 2010, the Mustang was slightly restyled, giving it an even more muscular look.

For the 2011 models, Ford redesigned all the engines in order to improve both horsepower and fuel-efficiency. Some of the engines allow the Mustang to get up to 31 miles (50 km) per gallon! Unlike the fuel-efficient Mustang II, the new Mustangs don't sacrifice power.

Starting in **2008**, Ford began using a soybean-based foam in the Mustang's seat cushions. The Ford Motor Company has used soybeans in their products for a long time. In **1941**, Ford built a car with plastic body panels made in part from soybeans.

This glass-roof Mustang appeals to fans of sunroofs. It lets light shine into the whole car.

Shelby Mustangs

   Almost since the first Mustang was sold, there have been people eager to alter their car's performance, appearance, or both. The most famous is Carroll Shelby. A legendary race-car driver in the 1950s, Carroll Shelby and his company, Shelby-American, began altering Mustangs in 1964. Ford asked Shelby for his help in developing a Mustang that could compete in the Sports Car Club of America (SCCA) road-racing series. The result was the 1965 Shelby GT350. The GT350 proved to be successful on the track, winning three straight SCCA national championships. It is now one of the most sought-after collector cars in the world.

INSIDE THE MACHINE

On the **45th** anniversary of the original, Shelby-American offered a brand-new edition of the **GT350**. In order to own a new Shelby **GT350**, customers first have to buy a **2011** Mustang **GT** from Ford, which costs about **$30,000**. Then they must send it to Shelby-American, who will transform it into a **GT350** for an additional **$33,995**. It's not cheap, but it's certainly fast!

This 2008 Shelby Mustang GT-C is pictured at the Las Vegas Motor Speedway.

Cultural Impact

The Mustang became one of the most important cars in American history. Today, there are about 250 Mustang car clubs across the world, the most for any car. The original Mustang can still be seen on roads, in garages, and at auto shows around the world. Amazingly, a 1965 Mustang in good condition can still be bought for less than $10,000.

Many car shows feature classic Ford Mustangs, inspiring new generations of pony-car fans everywhere.

The Ford Mustang has faced serious competition, but it has held its ground. The Mustang is the only pony car that has been in continuous production since its introduction. Others have come and gone, but the Mustang has remained.

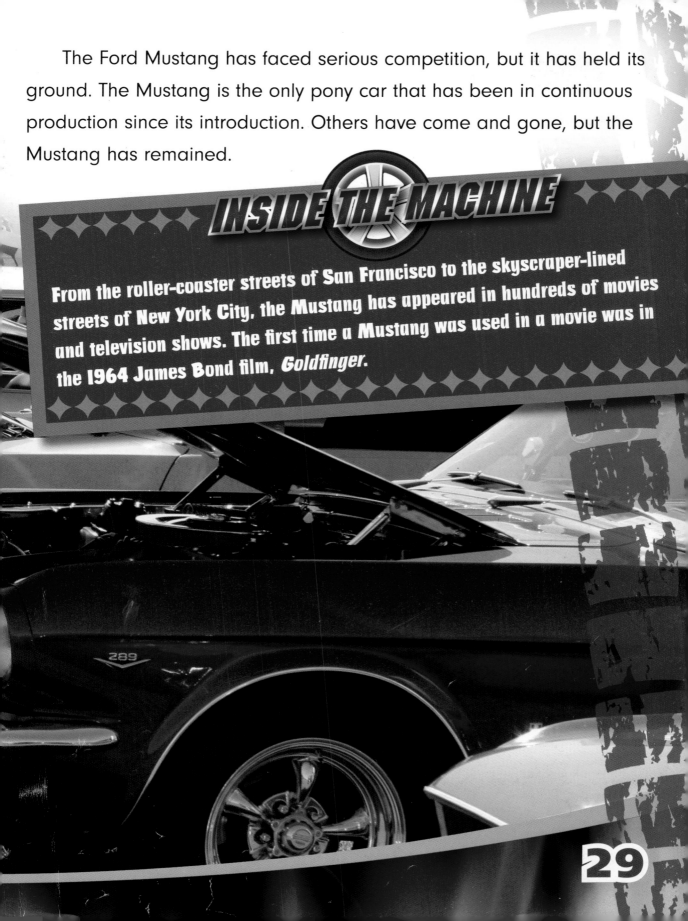

INSIDE THE MACHINE

From the roller-coaster streets of San Francisco to the skyscraper-lined streets of New York City, the Mustang has appeared in hundreds of movies and television shows. The first time a Mustang was used in a movie was in the 1964 James Bond film, *Goldfinger*.

Glossary

aerodynamic: having a shape that improves airflow around a car to increase its speed

big-block engine: a large engine produced in the 1960s and 1970s

convertible: a car with a roof that can be lowered or removed

coupe: a two-door car with one section for the seat and another for storage space

customize: to alter to fit someone's needs

designer: one who plans the pattern or shape of something

emblem: a sign that represents an object, idea, group, or quality

fuel-efficient: able to operate using little fuel, or without waste

grille: a metal screen on the front of a car that allows cool air into the engine

hatchback: a car in which the trunk lid is replaced by a hatch that usually includes the rear window

muscle car: a sports car with a powerful engine built for speed

platform sharing: using the same structure and many of the same parts to build a variety of different cars

spoiler: a wing-shaped device attached to the back of the car to improve airflow and stability

subcompact: a small car with limited passenger and luggage room

For More Information

Books

Maurer, Tracy. *Mustang*. Vero Beach, FL: Rourke Publishing, 2007.

Mueller, Mike. *The Complete Book of Mustang: Every Model Since 1964½*. St. Paul, MN: MBI Publishing, 2007.

Web Sites

Collisionkids.org
www.collisionkids.org
Learn about cars by playing games and completing related projects.

Ford Motor Company
www.ford.com
The official Ford Motor Company Web site features information about current Ford models, including the Mustang.

What's Inside: Muscle Cars
musclecars.howstuffworks.com
Learn about the mechanics of muscle cars, and see some classic examples.

Index